DIVERSITY STARTS WITH YOU

MARLON MOORE, Ph.D.

Self-n-Publish 30 DAYS
This Is The Year For Your New Book

WWW.SELFPUBLISHN30DAYS.COM

Published by *Self Publish -N- 30 Days*

Copyright 2021 Marlon Moore, Ph.D

All rights reserved worldwide. No part of this book may be reproduced or transmitted in any form or by any means electronic or mechanical, including photocopying, recording or by any information storage and retrieval system without written permission from Marlon Moore, Ph.D.

Printed in the United States of America

ISBN: 979-8-53117-571-7

1. Diversity 2. Organization 3. Inclusion 4. Guide

Disclaimer/Warning:
This book is intended for lecture and informative purposes only. This publication is designed to provide competent and reliable information regarding the subject matter covered. The author or publisher are not engaged in rendering legal or professional advice. Laws vary from state to state and if legal, financial, or other expert assistance is needed, the services of a professional should be sought. The author and publisher disclaim any liability that is incurred from the use or application of the contents of this book.

FOREWORD

When Marlon asked me to write this preface for his guidebook, I was both honored to be asked and deeply proud of the man he has become. I was first introduced to him when I taught as a professor in the graduate program on Diversity Management at Cleveland State University. As I watched him keep his distance from directly engaging, I whispered to him that he would learn more and have a more prominent impact if he got directly involved. He stepped forward and didn't look back.

I have been blessed to support Marlon as a mentor as he worked through personal and professional development through ever-increasing responsibility and impact in his chosen vocation of diversity, equity, and inclusion (DEI). This eventually led to the pinnacle of his corporate progression when he was named the chief diversity officer at Huntington Bank.

A new chapter in his career began when he stepped out of internal positions to establish his own consulting practice. In one of our conversations, it became clear it was time for him to stretch his reach to a larger audience.

I knew anyone who met him would recognize his personable and professional approach as clear, direct, and accessible. I am pleased Marlon chose to write a succinct and direct guide for developing a world-class diversity, equity, and inclusion strategy.

Regardless of the audience, it is well written, personable, and applicable. Moreover, I am delighted as his brevity lends the guide to be read by more organizational leaders. It will be apparent to these leaders that DEI is achievable and imperative in our amazingly diverse world. As one country at a time embraces diversity, equity, and inclusion, we all benefit from our growing humanity. The question for all readers is — because diversity starts with you are you ready to step in to engage DEI fully to make an impact?

Herb Stevenson
Cleveland Consulting Group, Inc.
CEO

DIVERSITY
INCLUSION
CHANGE
TEAM
EQUITY
people
years
society
inequality
States
workplace
America
American
moment
racism
look
may
power
supply
help
work
time
past
one
men
race
since
Powell
equal
need
last
fact
even
take
like
deep
part
white
areas

*This book is dedicated to those who are willing to take action
to make their workplace, community, and society
more diverse, equitable, and inclusive for all.*

CHANGE
DIVERSITY
INCLUSION
EQUITY
TEAM
racism
years
look
may
people
American
moment
work
one
States
inequality
society
race
men
since
power
supply
workplace
help
past
time
white
equal
need
fact
last
take
even
Powell
part
like
deep
Till
classism
dates
areas
get
act
1950
2009
1979
1920
1866
67
150
10450
20105
20106

ACKNOWLEDGMENTS

I want to thank all of you that have supported me, both personally and professionally. To my former colleagues, mentors, family, and friends — thank you so much for your inspiration, encouragement, and motivation. Special shout-out to Virginia State University, my undergraduate alma mater, and historically black college and university (HBCU) for shaping me as a student and man.

To Steve Steinour, president, chairman, and CEO of Huntington National Bank, thank you for believing in me and providing me the opportunity to serve as chief diversity and inclusion officer at Huntington.

If you are reading this book, I want to acknowledge and sincerely thank you for your support!

CHANGE
DIVERSITY
INCLUSION
TEAM
EQUITY
years
people
racism
look
may
even
equal
need
American
moment
white
time
work
past
one
inequality
States
race
society
since
power
supply
help
Powell
last
fact
take
like
deep
part
areas
men
workplace
America
Till
classism
dates

TABLE OF CONTENTS

Foreword

Introduction 1

PART I: Workplace Diversity 9
    Chapter One: Importance of Leadership 13
    Chapter Two: Drafting an Organizational DEI Policy Statement 23
    Chapter Three: Develop a DEI Operating Plan 29

PART II: Supplier Diversity 41
    Chapter Four: Key Components of Your Supplier Diversity Strategy 43
    Chapter Five: Supplier Development.. 53

Part III: Accountability 59
    Chapter Six: Establishing Accountability Metrics 61
    Chapter Seven: Establish an Internal Diversity Advisory Council 67
    Chapter Eight: Celebrate Progress.. 75
    Chapter Nine: Benchmark Best in Class Strategies and Initiatives 81

Conclusion 87

Ideas to Create an Inclusive and Equitable Workplace..........................91

Key Terms..95

Bibliography..97

DIVERSITY
INCLUSION
CHANGE
TEAM
EQUITY
society
inequality
States
people
American
years
look
racism
may
work
moment
time
past
help
power
supply
since
race
men
one
equal
need
Powell
fact
last
get
take
views
white
even
deep
like
part
areas
classism
Till
dates
1950
2009
1979
1920
1866
67
20105
20106
10450
150

INTRODUCTION

The history of the United States has a deep past clouded in suppression, classism, hierarchy, and racism. Slavery dates back over 400 hundred years. Anti-Asian bigotry in the country goes back over 150 years to when Chinese immigrants first arrived in California to help build the Transcontinental Railroad.[1] In 1950, Congress held hearings regarding the LGBT community in government, and three years later, President Dwight D. Eisenhower issued executive order 10450, banning homosexuals from government employment, including military service.[2]

If we're all part of the human race, why do people have racist attitudes? Why do we discriminate and act in hate? No race is superior or inferior to another, right?

A lot of our attitudes are shaped when we're young. When our family members or friends express racist opinions, it's common that we will take on those views ourselves. The problem is, unless we do something about it, these opinions can stay with us for a lifetime.

Quick disclaimer: this is not an anti-racism book. However, I feel it is appropriate to think about how our beliefs and attitudes about another group can reveal themselves in the workplace and serve as a barrier to the recruitment, development, or promotion of underrepresented groups or even the integration of diverse businesses as part of supply chains.

In the past, I have been asked numerous times, "What can I do to support underrepresented groups that continue to experience inequality?" For me, that is somewhat a very loaded question, but it does present an opportunity to continue the conversation of "why diversity starts with you."

As a DEI professional, I take these opportunities very seriously because it provides me a platform to engage in a dialogue that may bring about systemic change through deep introspection and reflection. Said differently, having a conversation about inequality, or more, in particular, equity, creates the space to discuss individual, group, and organizational actions that may promote a more

---

[1] Powell, 2021
[2] Powell, 2021

inclusive and equitable society. Our workplace practices, ideals and beliefs, and care for each other are key components to ensuring equity. So, my direct answer to 'What I can do?' is to take action. Create a DEI plan that addresses the many areas of opportunity we all have in the workplace to empower others and endure representation and access.

This book focuses on workplace actions that can promote the attraction, retention, and development of diverse talent and businesses. This is my life's work, and it is my hope that each of you reading this book will join me on the journey of creating a better workplace and society for all.

Many of us experienced the impact of the tragic losses in our society directly linked to racism such as Emmitt Till, Tamir Rice, and George Floyd.

Emmett Till, a 14-year-old African American from Chicago, IL was lynched in Mississippi in 1955 after being accused of offending a white woman by whistling at her in her family's grocery store.

Tamir Rice, a 12-year-old African American boy, was killed in my hometown of Cleveland, Ohio, by a 26-year-old white police officer for being in possession of a replica toy gun. Loehmann, the policeman, shot him almost immediately after arriving on the scene.

George Floyd, one of three African American men killed in the state of Minnesota by police. Mr. Floyd was killed during an arrest by former officer Derek Chauvin who knelt on his neck and back for 9 minutes and 29 seconds.

Unfortunately, I could probably finish this introduction by listing the countless names of those black and brown men and women who have died because of this intrinsic disease (racism).

In March 2021, several members of the Asian community were murdered in Atlanta, Georgia, by a white male that clearly had racist views toward that community. What fueled his motivation? What nurtured his anti-Asian American sentiment?

While it can be comforting to believe acts of violence are random evils, it is pertinent that we look not solely at the person committing hate crimes, but the environment that allowed that hatred to be fostered. When we think about why most organizations lack diversity at senior, executive, and board levels, we have to address what cultures are being created and subsequently nurtured within institutions that might demonstrate inequality in job and business opportunities.

I have been a diversity practitioner now for fifteen years. I've formally studied diversity management and lived in the South for a large chunk of my life. But nothing could have prepared me for the moment that I would personally experience racism.

I had spent forty-one years without incident and this jarring moment had a profound impact on my life. Nothing could have prepared me for it, but that moment prepared me for the days ahead.

I remember my life-changing experience vividly. It was a cold morning. The parking lot was empty except for my car. As I approached my vehicle, an idiot slowly drove by in his white pick-up and yelled at me, "Get away from the car, ni**er."

His voice reverberated off the adjacent buildings before he sped off. I looked to my left...then to my right, to make sure I was the focus of his racist comment.

> *I remember my life-changing experience vividly.*

As I stood in the empty lot, the reality set in that I was the target of his heinous remark. My blood started to boil, and my hands began to sweat as I slowly got in my car. He was gone, but the encounter left me wondering. Where might I see him again? Would he follow me home? Might this guy become someone I encounter again at the grocery store? Did we work together? The whole event left me emotional but not detoured.

At the time of this cowardly act, I was the chief diversity and inclusion officer (CDO) of a large Midwest bank. Here's the deal...it took being called a ni**er for me to really get off my tail and work my butt off to make a difference. Don't get me wrong, I was doing the work of a CDO, but that moment of being disrespected, profiled, and belittled made me want to do so much more to ensure a better society for everyone. workplace to empower others and endure representation and access.

As a matter of fact, it is the very reason why I am writing this book. I attribute the divide in our country to several things, but what I am most interested in is focusing on doing something about it. This book is designed to give you some of the tools you need to make a difference in your workplace.

If we include more minorities in our executive suites and supply chains, I firmly believe we will see a change in our education systems, healthcare, and wealth disparity. Over the last thirty years, wage inequality in the United States has increased substantially, with the overall inequality level now approaching the extreme lows that prevailed during the Great Depression.[3] Only college graduates have experienced growth in median weekly earnings since 1979.[4] High school dropouts have, by contrast, seen their median weekly earnings decline by about twenty-two percent.[5] High school dropout rates are least among whites and highest among Hispanics, while college enrollment rates are least among blacks and highest among whites.[6]

The incarceration rate in the United States has grown dramatically since the 1970s. The U.S. now has one of the highest rates in the world. The rise in incarceration has been especially prominent among young black males and high school dropouts.[7]

Before we begin to look at the inequality in our society, including corporate America, it is important to look at America's founding. Was there inequality in how things were written from the start? Were we all truly viewed as equal? In the entire history of the United States of America, we have only had one African American president and one woman vice president. Who had power, and was this power ever going to be relinquished? What inequalities have you experienced? How has that impacted how you view yourself and others

> **How has that impacted how you view yourself and others as equal?**

---

[3] Economic Policy Institute, 2011
[4] Bureau of Labor Statistics, 2009
[5] Bureau of Labor Statistics, 2009
[6] Economix, 2010
[7] Western, Bruce, and Becky, 2010

as equal? Even during the women's suffrage movement, women of color were discriminated against.

If I'm not mistaken, I read that in 1866, "All persons born or naturalized in the United States, and subject to the jurisdiction thereof, are citizens of the United States and of the State wherein they reside. No State shall make or enforce any law which shall abridge the privileges or immunities of citizens of the United States." For those who may not remember, the statement above is from our U.S. Constitution and the 14th Amendment. But years later, there was this concept/laws called "Jim "Crow" that segregated everything from schools, residential areas, theaters, pools, cemeteries to residential homes. My question is, in the eyes of those who founded this country and those who controlled many of its resources and power, were ethnic minorities ever considered equal with the rights and privileges of everyone else?

To understand where we need to go, we must spend a little time revisiting where we've come from. In his book, *The Business of Slavery and the Rise of American Capitalism*, historian Calvin Schermerhorn explains how slavery built America without returning virtually any of the gains to the enslaved people or their descendants.[8] He also describes how racial inequality is part of our national DNA and why it persists.

> If all men are to be created equal, change has to come.

Schermerhorn brilliantly tells the story of capitalist development through seven slave-trading firms and related enterprises. Its leading argument is that the business of slavery in the early U.S. republic charts the development of capitalism in terms of chains of credit and commodities, organization, and technology. He would also contend that "slave-traders. . .created integrated systems of supply and credit that anticipate concepts like vertical integration and supply chain management a century later." The sobering reality is we must remember the past, but we can't stay there.

Yes, my ancestors helped build this country. In fact, during a recent trip to Georgia to uncover my family lineage, I discovered my great-great grand-

---

[8] Schermerhorn, 2015

father's gravesite. He passed away on August 18, 1920, in Madison, Georgia. Even as he worked to pave the way for his Ph.D. grandson, he struggled to push past social barriers. While everyone must earn their place in this world, minorities in America usually line up fifty yards behind the starting line. If all men are to be created equal, change has to come. This is where you and I come in.

Cornelius Vanderbilt, John D. Rockefeller, Andrew Carnegie, J.P. Morgan, and Henry Ford are names synonymous with innovation and big business in America. They have all built empires and created advances in technology. They helped shape the country in its early days by doing things such as developing the models for modern railroads, creating the modern financial system, and making cars accessible to the masses.[9] You may be wondering what this has to do with diversity. Slavery, capitalism, power, privilege, bias are all constructs that have been in existence since 1492.

To break them will take intrinsic self-motivation to change the fabric of our society. That's if we really want to. What if blacks received their forty acres and a mule? Would we have more Moore's, Jenkins, and Smith's like we did the Carnegies, Kennedy's, and Vanderbilt's?

This book is designed to help level that playing field. I will introduce you to basic concepts that will help you and your organization succeed in creating a workforce that reflects the changing demographics of society, drives economic inclusion, and closes the income and health inequality gaps by providing those underrepresented groups with meaningful opportunities to create, and thus pass on generational wealth.

As Cornelius Vanderbilt and John D. Rockefeller are names synonymous with innovation and big business in America, it is time to change the narrative and create a society that lists new names like yours and mine that will accelerate a more equitable future for all.

No need to look any further than the highest office in the land to determine if we can pull this off. President Joe Biden has provided us with a very simple

---

[9] Schermerhorn, 2015

roadmap. Does Joe know something we don't? Currently, it appears that 67% of his nominees and appointees, including the Vice President-Elect of the United States, are gender or ethnically diverse.[10]

If you include other dimensions of diversity such as age, sexual orientation, and wealth status, the number is even higher! Some may say, "He's only appointing people that he knows." Maybe, but notice how they are not all white men. Then go a little further in your assessment. Look who he knows. It's actually not hard to reflect "the people."

Diversity really starts with you.

Diversity really starts with *you*. It begins with your willingness to diversify your network. Your willingness to build meaningful relationships with people who don't look like you. Your willingness to give someone with different abilities the opportunity to flourish. Your willingness to close the income equality gap by promoting economic inclusion. If your personal life is full of a myriad of different people, you'll find your professional life lifts up the same.

---

[10] NPR, 2021

CHANGE
DIVERSITY
INCLUSION
EQUITY
TEAM
racism
years
look
may
people
American
equal
need
fact
last
get
Powell
moment
white
time
work
past
one
inequality
States
society
since
power
supply
help
race
men
part
like
deep
take
big
views
even
areas
racist
now
Till
classism
dates
2009
1950
1920
1979
150
10450
1866
67
20105
20106
400

PART I
WORKPLACE DIVERSITY

"To thine own self be true."
— *William Shakespeare*

DIVERSITY
CHANGE
INCLUSION
TEAM
EQUITY
society
years
people
racism
look
may
work
one
inequality
States
workplace
America
American
equal
moment
time
past
power
since
race
men
take
need
Powell
last
fact
get
even
areas
white
part
like
deep
supply
help
views
1950
2009
1979
1920
1866
150
10450
20105
20106
67
classism
Till
dates

Definition of Diversity, Equity, and Inclusion

Diversity, equity, and inclusion are separate yet interconnected ideals that often work in tandem but seek different objectives. The significant work of DEI will be guided by these principles and strengthened by the involvement and support of each of us.

- **Diversity** is the representation of varied identities and differences (race, ethnicity, gender, disability, sexual orientation, gender identity, national origin, socio-economic status, thinking and communication styles, etc.), collectively and as individuals.

$$\text{Diversity = Representation}$$

- **Equity** seeks to ensure fair treatment, equality of opportunity, and fairness in access to information and resources for all. This is highly possible in an environment built on trust, respect, and dignity.

$$\text{Equity = Access}$$

- **Inclusion** builds a culture of belonging by actively inviting the contribution and participation of all people. Every person's voice adds value and creates balance in the face of power differences.

$$\text{Inclusion = Empowerment}$$

Civil Rights Imperative → Affirmative Action → Managing Diversity and Inclusion → DEI as a Strategic Business Imperative

Continuum of Organizational Diversity Work

Many of us have heard the statement, "Diversity drives performance, innovation, and leads to better outcomes for organizations."[11] Yet, ethnic minorities and women still lag in the number of executive and senior level roles. Consider this, according to the data from the Association of American Medical Colleges, the University of Maryland, Baltimore County produces more black M.D. and Ph.D. degree earners than any other college in the country. That suggests there are very talented people in our society capable of achieving amazing things if given the same support as the majority and that the University of Maryland has done a great job of uplifting underrepresented students.

But diverse representation is not enough. Organizations must create a workplace environment where people from underrepresented groups feel included and empowered. When was the last time you saw an ethnic minority or woman be given the opportunity to lead a critical project? Have you sought input or feedback recently from someone diverse? These are all behaviors that lead to inclusion.

I will never forget the time when I was in a room with the top executives from a company and the CEO personally asked me what I thought about the language we were using as a company and whether we should consider something different. It was not my response that made the difference for me, but the feeling of empowerment that made me feel not only included as a colleague but a leader of the company.

Once we make advancements with representation (diversity) and empowerment (inclusion), then it's time to provide access (equity). Listen, I have seen it firsthand. To make decisions, you not only need a seat and voice at the table, but someone has to grant you access to the room. Sponsoring someone and seeing that they have all the resources and tools to succeed goes a long way to ensuring equity and access as you go through talent planning.

Think about someone diverse in your organization that has consistently performed at a high level and give them secrets — oops, I meant tools — to thrive at your company. Listen, let's be honest here. Some places you need to be invited into.

---

[11] Byrd and Scott, 2018

CHAPTER 1

IMPORTANCE OF LEADERSHIP

Success in the workplace often occurs when individuals are more aware of the impact of personal experiences on their professional and personal lives.[12] Self-awareness provides a deep understanding of one's emotions, strengths, weaknesses, needs, and drives.[13] People who demonstrate high levels of self-awareness recognize the impact of their emotions at work and home. Individuals hold certain schemas or traits used to define effective leadership.[14]

How many times have you gone through the workday and paused to think through a behavior or emotion? I would imagine fairly often. Congratulations! You were experiencing self-awareness – an effective leadership trait.

I vividly recall the 2016 mass shooting at a gay nightclub in Orlando, Florida. My first thought was of my colleagues from the LGBTQ and how they felt. Just this year, there was a shooting at a FedEx warehouse in Indianapolis. I have a client with a considerable workforce in Indiana. I immediately thought about how their associates' families may have been impacted. I didn't know them personally, but that didn't stop me from sending a note to the CEO expressing my awareness of the situation and my consideration for all those involved. Being more aware of your personal experiences and demonstrating more empathy even for people you may not have a direct relationship with is a key practice in DEI work.

Over the years, scholars, trainers, and human resource professionals have determined that emotional intelligence is a fundamental leadership trait that distinguishes high performers in an organization.[15] All emotions are valid on the job and convey information critical to understanding performance.[16] A key domain

---

[12] Urdang, 2010; Showry & Manasa, 2014
[13] Goleman, 2004
[14] Lord, 1985; Nichols & Contrell, 2014
[15] Caruso, 1999
[16] Caruso, 1999; Sok, et al., 2014

of emotional intelligence (EI) is self-awareness. Success in the workplace often occurs when individuals are more aware of the impact of personal experiences on their professional and personal lives.[17]

Self-awareness represents the foundational domain of EI. This helps guide how we view ourselves in relation to others and ultimately become our authentic selves.[18] Self-awareness provides a deep understanding of one's emotions, strengths, weaknesses, needs, and drives.[19]

People who demonstrate high levels of self-awareness recognize the impact of their emotions at work and home. Duval & Wicklund describe self-awareness as the ability to understand the link between feelings and what we do, think, or say.[20] To increase self-awareness, one must begin with self-acceptance. Movement toward self-acceptance is recognizing that emotions are real and should not be assigned a negative value of right or wrong.

DEI work extends beyond the workplace. We all have an opportunity to ensure equity in our communities. That's what makes us stronger together. If an elderly black woman needs help cutting her grass, will you extend a helping hand? When you see someone being mistreated by another person, will you speak up? What would you want someone to do if someone in a position of power was mistreating your child?

People who demonstrate high levels of self-awareness recognize the impact of their emotions at work and home.

Self-awareness is a powerful leadership trait. Early self-awareness research showed that heightened self-focus has the main effect on attributions; self-focused people saw themselves as more responsible for both positive and negative events.[21] In the theories described above, self-awareness is demonstrated through one's ability to recognize the impact of experiences at the moment (simple conscious awareness).

---

[17] Showry & Manasa, 2014; Urdang, 2010
[18] Goleman, 1995
[19] Goleman, 2004
[20]; Goleman, 1998
[21] Duval & Wicklund, 1973

In order to assess the impact or make meaning of the recognition of consciousness, one has to reflect or possess the ability to stand apart from and evaluate behaviors, beliefs, or feelings.[22] Since self-awareness is a vital trait in good leaders, how can leadership aid in diversity, equity, and inclusion? I'm so glad you asked.

Self-awareness represents a soft skill that carries significant meaning when recognizing and understanding the impact of behavior, beliefs, and experiences.[23] This is an essential tool in understanding the power of understanding and modeling inclusive leadership behaviors.

> *Inclusive leaders articulate a genuine commitment to DEI without being prompted.*

Inclusive leaders articulate a genuine commitment to DEI without being prompted. It's how they operate, inspire, and encourage every day. They challenge the status quo and hold others accountable in making DEI intrinsically motivating.

There are at least four traits or behaviors that distinguish inclusive leaders from others.

- **Empowerment:** Provides context that enables others to solve problems and do their best work. Inclusive leaders empower others, pay attention to the diversity of thinking and psychological safety, and focus on team cohesion.
- **Humility:** Fosters open communication, learning from the different views of others, and accepting and respectful of differences. Inclusive leaders are modest about capabilities, admit mistakes, and create the space for others to contribute. They listen without judgment and demonstrate empathy to understand those around them.
- **Courage:** This is needed to demonstrate a willingness to show your "why" and expand comfort zones even when the outcome is uncertain. Inclusive leaders show awareness of personal blind spots as well as flaws in the system and work hard to ensure equity.

---

[22] Boyatzis, Stubbs, & Taylor, 2002; Kondrat, 1999
[23] Kondrat, 1999

- **Accountability:** Be responsible for modeling the behaviors you expect of others. It is essential to hold individuals responsible for the way they perform. Inclusive leaders are committed to action and regularly conduct discussions at all levels of an organization regarding DEI.

These traits may seem obvious or similar to those that are broadly needed for effective leadership, but the difference between assessing and developing quality leadership versus inclusive leadership lies in specific action.

Inclusive leadership is not about occasional grand gestures but regular, smaller-scale comments and actions. Inclusive leaders take time to grow and learn. They take ownership of their awareness of social and cultural norms, and they do it in a way that is truly authentic and trusting.

> *Inclusive leaders take time to grow and learn.*

Diversity, equity, and inclusion are at the forefront of most conversations today in society, specifically in business across all industries. PwC, for example, has led the charge with the CEO Action for Diversity and Inclusion, which the largest CEO-driven business commitment of its kind ever made. Organizations like Starbucks and McDonalds have also announced the DEI will be tied to executive compensation, a suggested best practice.[24] There have been more diverse job postings than I thought I would ever see. Shucks, the current state of affairs is what motivated me to launch my consulting practice.

But why is workplace diversity important? DEI has become more than just something a company can check off a list; it has grown into a movement, or said more appropriately, a strategic business imperative that — when executed correctly — can have a direct effect on a company's bottom line.

It's not about affirmative action but leveraging the unique ability, talent, and differences of others to drive performance. Today, it is more necessary than ever to create a work environment that displays these tenets and integrates them as part of their core values and business models.

---

[24] Deloitte, 2017

Whether your colleagues are members of the LGBTQ+ community, belong to minority groups based on gender or ethnicity, or come from a variety of different educational or cultural backgrounds, it is imperative they feel included and supported in the day-to-day workplace for their personal successes, as well as those of the company. Inclusion creates a sense of belonging and commitment to the organizational values and mission.

Companies increasingly rely on diverse, multidisciplinary teams that combine the collective capabilities of women and men, people of different cultural heritage, and younger and older workers. But simply throwing a mix of people together doesn't guarantee high performance; it requires inclusive leadership — leadership that assures that all team members feel they are treated respectfully and fairly, are valued and sense that they belong, and are confident and inspired.

Inclusive behaviors in the workplace, especially when modeled by leaders, can unlock the innovative potential of a diverse workforce, enabling companies to increase not only their share of existing markets but also brand-new open ones. Diversity, equity, and inclusion enable unique thinking and improved decision-making through a more profound and comprehensive worldview.

I was leading a group session of primarily white men, and I noticed that the women weren't speaking up at all on the topic at hand. From my perspective, they were clearly knowledgeable of the subject matter, but the men were the only ones speaking.

As an inclusive leader, what was I supposed to do? How could I get their voice in the room? To switch things up, I had all the participants stand up and move to a different table. I then asked each table to talk about the topic and I would randomly choose someone to report out (smile). Needless to say, we heard from a number of women over the next twenty minutes. The point is sometimes we have to be purposeful about ensuring various groups are represented.

So, what roles do you have in ensuring a diverse, inclusive, and equitable workplace? Creating a diverse and inclusive workplace requires us to take ownership of creating a competitive, innovative, and empowering approach not just to our financial bottom-line but to our societal consciousness as well.

In his book, *Find Your Why*, Simon Sinek brilliantly talks about the importance and process for finding clarity, meaning, and fulfillment. It is imperative that we live in alignment with our purpose, and this starts with gaining clarity of our "why."

Lucky for you, I'm not going to ask you to write up a book report, but I will ask you to think about this question. Why is DEI important to you? Often times we hear leaders say that it is "the right thing to do." However, I would argue that representation, empowerment, and having equitable access to resources that allow us to close the racial and equality gap in our country goes deeper than just "doing the right thing."

Ensuring diversity, equity, and inclusion starts with an intrinsic motivation to leave society better than you found it. Now that you have at least begun thinking about why DEI is important to you, let's take a look at what can get in the way of our desire to lead inclusively.

> Ensuring diversity, equity, and inclusion starts with an intrinsic motivation to leave a better society than you found.

In order for a person to be able to function in their environment, they need some form of a guiding philosophy that allows them to make sense of their world and to interact with it. All inquisitive beings naturally have questions about the world and seek answers to those questions in order to live an adequate life. The set of answers a person has to the philosophical questions that are essential to life constitutes the person's worldview.

A worldview is a consistent and integral sense of existence and provides a framework for generating, sustaining, and applying knowledge. Literally, a worldview is how a person views the world. A person's worldview consists of the values, ideas, or fundamental belief system that determines his or her attitudes, beliefs, and ultimately, actions.

What is your worldview on DEI? Do you view DEI as a compliance exercise (or just another thing to do because someone said so), or do you truly believe that diversity, equity, and inclusion give your organization a competitive advantage?

How does embracing differences make us a better society? Is it possible that if we intentionally seek to place more minorities in leadership roles with competitive salaries that we can begin to close the income inequality gap in our country? If you gave any of these questions the requisite attention they deserve, then you are on your way to shifting your paradigm on DEI.

At my former employer, I remember facilitating a DEI discussion with a group of executive leaders (most were white males). During that session, I conducted an exercise where I asked everyone to examine their networks by thinking about how many people they knew, regularly interacted with, or got services from that were diverse.

Something extraordinary happened from that exercise. A few weeks later, I received a call from the senior executive in the group. He told me, "The exercise really made me think about who my friends are and who I regularly interact with. I've noticed that very few are diverse." He was humbled and wanted to change. So, he decided to start with me. This led to us (me, him, and his wife) taking a two-hour trip to my hometown, visiting my former high school, neighborhood, and meeting my friends and family. We even went to a club.

Listen, I'm sure some of you all are reading this and thinking, "Marlon, that was a nice gesture (*blah-blah-blah*). Who wants to feel like a charity case (*blah-blah-blah*)? But it was nothing like that for me. The moment this white guy recognized that he had very few black friends and wanted to take immediate action to change was an act of humility and courage. The fact that he chose me was empowering.

I felt like I found that "something" that I could use to build a genuine friendship upon. He was someone who could mentor me. He was someone that I could have challenging conversations with. He was someone I could work with to change the narrative of what we see and experience in society.

Six months later, when he invited me to his house, we had the most authentic time. Trust was established as a bond was nurtured. I earned a new friend and ally in this fight for inclusion and equity.

What leaders say and do can have a significant impact on others. Subtle words and acts of exclusion by leaders or overlooking the exclusive behaviors of others can easily reinforce the behavior we don't need or want to see. Diversity has to be active, and you cannot see the results you want with a passive attitude.

It takes energy and deliberate effort to create an inclusive culture. That starts with leaders paying much more attention to what they say and making daily adjustments as necessary. Will everyone drive two hours and meet you and your friends? Maybe not, but as an inclusive leader, take the action that is impactful and achievable for you, and do it often.

> *It takes energy and deliberate effort to create an inclusive culture.*

There's more to be learned about how to become an inclusive leader and harness the power of diverse teams. Still, one thing is clear: leaders who consciously practice inclusive leadership and actively develop their capability will see the results in the superior performance of their diverse teams.

As an inclusive leader, I am intrinsically motivated to change the world by delivering practical and leading-edge solutions that empower diverse talent, build inclusive leaders, and foster innovative and equitable cultures. As you continue to lead inclusively, remind yourself daily of what matters to you. Tell others; communication is key. Lead by understanding and living your "why."

DEI GUIDED QUESTIONS

These questions are designed for you to reflect on what you read in this chapter and answer as appropriate.

1. Do you consider yourself a self-aware leader?

___

2. Do you model inclusive leadership behaviors?

___

3. Do you empower people from underrepresented groups? If so, how?

___

4. Is your team at work diverse? If not, why?

___

5. Do you live in a diverse community? If not, why?

___

JOURNAL SECTION

CHAPTER 2

DRAFTING AN ORGANIZATIONAL DEI POLICY STATEMENT

If you have taken an Organizational Behavior course or participated in an organized activity, you have seen levels of influence. The three levels of influence are at the individual, group, and organization levels. In the previous chapter, we described how DEI could be advanced at the individual level by inclusive leadership. Now, let's take a look at how we can ensure even more development through influence at the organizational level.

What is going to set the tone for your DEI strategy? What can both internal and external stakeholders refer to when seeking to understand what matters to your organization? What statement can you refer to when times get hard? These questions should all be in your organizational DEI statement.

A DEI statement demonstrates a company's commitment to building an inclusive, varied workplace that is welcoming to people of all backgrounds. Much like a mission and values statement, the DEI statement is, ideally, more than just a marketing exercise. It should guide your hiring, employee benefits, customer service, and workplace culture.

Some organizations tend to want to omit "policy," and that is a subtle preference. Policy can be interpreted as a mandate. DEI should never feel like a program or initiative that you're being told to do. DEI should be an integrated business imperative that you believe will help your company drive performance. That being said, whether your stated commitment to this work reads like a "policy" or "commitment" statement, the focus should always be having a DEI statement that inspires and clearly articulates that DEI matters to your organization.

Your DEI statement should answer three central questions:
- What is important?
- Why is it important?
- Who is responsible?

While addressing these three questions, the statement should align with your core organizational values and principles. It should also be signed by your most senior executive leader, usually the chief executive officer (CEO).

As you approach drafting your DEI statement, it is vital to understand the impact you can have with this document. Authenticity and intentionality must be at the very foundation of your statement. Authenticity creates a path for everyone and a direction. If you just include buzzwords or align your statement to a current event, there may not be anything to anchor into or connect with as possible.

> *Authenticity creates a path for everyone and a direction.*

A respectable DEI statement triangulates with your company's mission, vision, and values and is usually no more than three paragraphs in length. What do you want to say about your business? What do you want employees and customers to know about your commitment to DEI?

Lastly, whether you communicate your organizational position on DEI as a policy statement, commitment statement, or just post it as a letter from the CEO, be sure to share a draft with internal stakeholders such as an employee resource group, a DEI Advisory Council, and maybe even members of your board of directors. Buy-in and affording others an opportunity to weigh in on this subject is important.

Your statement should inspire and motivate others to lead authentically. It should attract candidates to your organization because it shows where your company's priorities lie on the DEI continuum.

Example: Pelotonia started as an idea. A ride. A weekend. To make a difference. To make an impact. Founded in 2008, Pelotonia was established with the objective to fund innovative cancer research. Pelotonia is a three-day experience that includes a weekend of cycling, entertainment, and volunteerism. But Pelotonia was never just about the ride. It's always been about setting and achieving an ambitious goal and raising critical funds to fight a disease that impacts us all.

At Pelotonia, we put people first. Not just some people, but all people. We fund innovative cancer research, and we are deeply committed to ensuring that this is done in an equitable and inclusive way.

We are committed to diversity, equity, and inclusion (DEI) and will continually work to improve the diversity of our board, team, supplier base, community, and research investments. Creating an environment where everyone has equal opportunities stimulates innovation, presents new approaches, and brings fresh perspectives that allow us to expand our work into more diverse communities and make a meaningful impact in the lives of others. Our participants, donors, investors, and partners must engage in active contribution to a diverse community — unified in our shared pursuit of ending cancer.

Your statement should inspire and motivate others to lead authentically.

To accomplish this, we must do the work.

We have identified four key pillars where we feel we can have our greatest impact: supplier diversity, workforce diversity, community engagement, and research investment. Our strategies and actions will push us to progress in each of these crucial areas of focus. We will establish Pelotonia as a national leader by how we spend with our suppliers, recruit and develop our workforce, build our community, and how we invest in innovative cancer research. Because we know that diversity enables excellence and innovation that can only be realized through a healthy collaboration of different ideas, experiences, and perspectives.

We look forward to doing this work and continuing to build a community for all committed to One Goal.

Doug Ulman
Pelotonia
President and CEO

Pelotonia did a really great job of developing a statement that reflects their core values while articulating why DEI is important and who is responsible. Equally as important, they were very clear about the areas of focus that would drive the change they want to see (supplier and workforce diversity, community engagement, and research investments).

As you consider developing or refining your organizational statement, be clear, concise, and resolute regarding what you expect from your colleagues. [25]

---
[25] This will serve you well as you begin executing your overall DEI strategy.

DEI GUIDED QUESTIONS

These questions are designed for you to reflect on what you read in this chapter and answer as appropriate.

1. Does your organization have a stated commitment to DEI?

___

2. Does your statement inspire you and lead to action that promotes DEI?

___

3. Why is this work important to you at an individual and organizational level?

___

4. Who do you ultimately believe is responsible for improving diversity, equity, and inclusion at your company?

___

5. Does your company have clear areas of focus for DEI?

___

JOURNAL SECTION

CHAPTER 3

DEVELOPING A DEI OPERATING PLAN

Now that we are intrinsically motivated and have a commitment and policy statement that reminds us of DEI's significance, we need to operationalize the words we just committed to in the previous chapter. I have had a number of organizations reach out to me wanting to know "how to move beyond words." My response? At some point, most companies started with a business plan.

A business plan is significant because it allows an organization the ability to lay out their goals and track improvement over time. A DEI operating plan is not very different from an organization's business plan. A DEI operating plan allows an organization to set very specific strategic objectives that can be measured to ensure growth related to representation, inclusion, or access. This allows companies to move beyond training to actually develop a strategy that promotes progress.

Much like most business plans, creating a DEI plan forces you to sit down and think about your major areas of opportunity before you get started. This includes your workforce demographics, spend with diverse companies, marketing collateral, and even what products you'll sell. Building a sustainable DEI plan begins with asking the right questions.

A few questions could be:
- What do we want to focus on?
- How are we going to go about doing it?
- What are our strategic objectives?
- Who needs to be involved in the process?

Asking these questions or questions similar to these ensures that the strategy will align with the right objectives and needs of the business. Most notably, having an operating plan helps you make meaningful steps toward diversity, equity, and inclusion. Your operating plan will consist of key areas of focus that should help improve your workforce, supplier base, or simply areas of influence. You can change what organizations you support financially. You can change or update policies or procedures that support military deployment benefits, gender identity, or promotions to include a more diverse candidate slate.

> *Resist the urge to immediately set goals.*

Resist the urge to immediately set goals. You will get there. Instead, really focus on the content of your operating plan. Take the information that you may have gained from focus groups, surveys, and benchmarking best practices and use that to inform your operating plan.

Even if you already have a DEI plan, you should visit your operating plan annually, but much of the content should remain consistent year to year. A strong DEI strategy can take three to five years to mature, so give yourself some time to see improvement before making significant changes. You will add components over time. This may include new resource groups and additional training resources.

> *Improving the diversity of your executive leadership team might constitute progress.*

You may even begin to track other dimensions of diversity in your workforce beyond gender and race (i.e., sexual orientation, military status, etc.). The point is to stay focused on your core objectives until you see progress.

Improving the diversity of your executive leadership team might constitute progress. Improving your spend with minority-owned businesses is another reliable measure of progress. Lastly, seeing improvement in colleague engagement is another major way to measure evolution with DEI. The remainder of this chapter will focus on several areas essential to building a world-class DEI strategy and operating plan.

DEI Policy Statement

Remember the policy statement we just referenced in the previous chapter? Every operating plan should begin with a statement that communicates to internal and external parties why DEI is important to the organization. Your policy statement creates a path and direction. Simply embed a copy of your statement within your operating plan.

Along with including it in your operating plan, make sure your statement is posted and easily accessible on your company's website. Potential candidates, investors, and community partners will often search for this commitment without you ever knowing they did so. Including this statement in your operating plan is a constant reminder of why DEI matters.

> *Your policy statement creates a path and direction.*

DEI Strategic Objectives

Your strategic objectives are the areas that you want to focus on. Some organizations will seek to improve the attraction and promotion of diverse talent, support diverse organizations, or drive economic inclusion through supplier diversity.

Whichever you decide, don't try to "boil the ocean" or take on too much at one time. Make sure your objectives align with your business model and can be executed in a timely manner.

Be sure to socialize the proposed objectives with internal leaders and stakeholders to ensure that you have buy-in and alignment. Also, make sure you can effectively measure how you improve against the stated objectives.

EXAMPLE OF STRATEGIC OBJECTIVES

1. WORKFORCE DIVERSITY

2. COMMUNITY ENGAGEMENT

3. SUPPLIER DIVERSITY

EXAMPLE OF STRATEGIC OBJECTIVES WITH GOALS AND INITIATIVES

{ - Improve ethnic and gender diversity in senior leadership roles by 15%.
  - Update langage with recruiting firms.

{ - Invest $1.5 million dollars with organizations that research health disparities for ethnic minorities.

{ - Spend 15% of our total procurement with diverse businesses.
  - Conduct at least two forums.

Build an organizational scorecard that allows for transparency, accountability, and review of progress.

At this point, diversity awareness is everything. Both internal and external partners should be made aware of your focus, and everyone should be behind the plan. Below we will take a look at other components that can be included as part of your overall DEI plan. These initiatives alone do not represent a best in class DEI strategy, but they do offer key activities that provide you with a formidable foundation when leveraged together.

DEI Training

DEI training is not the end-all, be-all! I repeat, please do not use DEI training as the only way to address this strategic business imperative within your organization.

Any world-class DEI strategy balances the use of training and strategic objectives that help your organization move the needle (e.g., workforce, supplier diversity, etc.). Training should be used to build awareness, engage in discussion, and introduce language and terms that create a more inclusive and equitable workforce. Additionally, be sure to balance online learning versus in-person learning.

There is no substitute for sitting across from another person and really getting a sense of what they think or feel. In-person training, when conducted by a DEI professional, can build community and a deeper understanding of the subject matter. DEI doesn't happen in silos. It requires the cooperation of everyone at the organization to be successful.

In particular, managers are hugely influential in how these initiatives are carried out. That's why it's important to invest in management training to help them understand what the company's diversity goals are, why they're needed, and what's expected of them when they interact with employees. Remember the inclusive leadership behavior? It only takes one person to display insensitive or non-inclusive behavior to taint the company's culture and an employee's experience.

Affinity Groups

Many organizations use different terms for these groups (network, business, employee, or affinity groups). They began as small, informal, self-started employee groups for people with common interests. These groups create an environment where everyone has equal opportunities, stimulates innovation, presents new approaches, and brings fresh perspectives that allow your organization to expand work into more diverse communities and make a meaningful impact in the lives of others. While these groups focus on common interests, affinity groups should not be exclusive.

At my previous company (before becoming the chief diversity officer), I remember joining a women's business resource group (even though I am a black male). This was very rewarding for me because I was able to see the corporate environment through someone else's eyes.

I learned about some of the challenges women face in the workplace, and because of that experience, I committed to being an ally for change. Together we were able to make enhancements to our caregiver time off policy and mother's rooms. Inclusive leaders demonstrate an open mindset and deep curiosity and seek to understand those around them.

> *Inclusive leaders demonstrate an open mindset and deep curiosity and seek to understand those around them.*

However you structure your groups, the format should assist with the execution of the overall business case for DEI and extend the organizational reach by increasing shared responsibility.

Meetings should occur at least once a month and provide an ongoing platform to discuss strategic objectives, progress, challenges, and goal attainment. Additionally, the groups can ensure the planning and execution of volunteer events, speaker series, or professional development.

Group operating principles should:

- Consist of a voluntary group led by colleagues.

- Have activities that align to the strategic objectives or overall DEI commitment.
- Exemplify membership and participation, representing all colleagues.

Best in class organizations take an active interest in their employee/business resource groups. Oftentimes, the chief executive officer will meet with group leadership to review the business plan and remove potential roadblocks.

Affinity groups should serve as an extension of your DEI team. They are provided an annual budget and executive sponsor to advance the DEI strategies.

Diversity, Equity & Inclusion Pipeline Strategy

The DEI talent pipeline strategy is designed to complement and support the efforts of the overall talent acquisition strategy.

Talent acquisition (TA) is a multi-faceted approach that should focus on the following:

- **Colleague Referrals** – Through personal networks or through relationship-building at external events, *all* colleagues should seek to meet diverse talent. This should not be just the focus of the TA or the DEI team. Sometimes employees are the best recruiters!
- **Identify Top Search Firms for Diverse Talent** – In the event their searches require the services of a third party, engage search firms that specialize in sourcing diverse talent. Also, make sure you have language in your contract that requires a percentage of referrals to be diverse (e.g., ethnicity, gender, sexual orientation, etc.).
- **Partner with Diverse Organizations** – Partner with professional, undergraduate/collegiate, black & Hispanic fraternities and sororities, and historically black colleges and universities to improve your diverse talent pipeline. The current vice president of the United States, Kamala Harris, is a graduate of an HBCU.

To continue to attract diverse talent, companies should build relationships with recruiting firms and organizations that support the advancement and development of various diverse constituents. Below are a few suggestions. However, I encourage your organization to conduct the proposed due diligence to find partners who meet your needs.

- Executive Leadership Council (ELC)   www.elcinfo.com
- Professional Diversity Network   www.prodivnet.com
- Prospanica   www.prospanica.org
- Military Talent Source   www.militarytalentsource.com

DEI Communication Plan

Communication is one of the most critical steps in implementing and managing an effective DEI strategy. My mantra is, "Communicate authentically and often."

Keeping your colleagues aware of what actions and initiatives are taking place promotes accountability and buy-in (at all levels of the organization). Take moments to celebrate cultural and heritage celebrations.

When successfully implemented, a communication plan will do the following:

- Increase awareness.
- Educate employees on your commitment to the DEI.
- Generate interest and increase participation with the affinity groups.

To gauge the effectiveness of an operating and communication plan, consider the following:

- Add DEI to your employee engagement survey to measure improvement and seek feedback.
- Measure the amount of "hits" to your internal and external diversity page.
- Monitor comments or thoughts shared by your employees and customers on social media.

Additional communication items for consideration:

- Vendor Policy
- Supplier Diversity Profile Form (to be distributed at external events)
- Annual Report
- Dedicated DEI page on an external website

External Advertorial Opportunities:

- DEI focused publications
- Local media publications

Below is a list (not all-inclusive) of heritage months and cultural celebrations for your organization to consider:

- January: MLK Day of Service (Jan. 18), International Holocaust Remembrance Day (Jan. 27)
- February: Black History Month
- March: National Women's History Month, International Women's Day (Mar. 8)
- April: Good Friday (Apr. 2), Easter (Apr. 4), Ramadan begins (Apr .12)
- May: Asian Pacific American Heritage Month, Eid al-Fitr (May 12)
- June: Pride Month, Juneteenth (June 19)
- July: Eid al-Adha (July 19)
- August: Women's Equality Day (Aug. 26)
- September: National Hispanic-Latinx Heritage Month (Sept. 15)
- October: National Disability Employment Awareness Month, National Immigrants Day (Oct. 28)
- November: National American Indian Heritage Month, Diwali (Nov. 4), Veteran's Day (Nov. 11), Hanukkah begins
- December: Christmas (Dec. 25), Kwanzaa begins (Dec. 26)

When building your communications strategy, be sure to engage the following internal partners: Communications/Marketing, Legal, Human Resources, and members of your affinity groups.

Best in class organizations leverage an effective internal and external communications strategy to gain market share by tapping into the purchasing power of diverse groups.

A final piece to your operating plan should include a focus on supplier diversity. A vital part of decreasing the income and wealth gap in American is supporting businesses owned by ethnic minorities, women, and other underrepresented groups.

As you finalize your plan, focus on the major components to supplier diversity that will spur economic inclusion and integrate diverse businesses into your supply chain (see chapter 5).

DEI GUIDED QUESTIONS

These questions are designed for you to reflect on what you read in this chapter and answer as appropriate.

1. Does your organization have a DEI operating plan?

___

2. What areas of opportunity do you see for your company to improve its DEI efforts?

___

3. Do you currently hire employees or spend dollars within your organization? If so, how do you ensure a diverse workforce and supplier base?

___

4. Are there specific parts of the DEI operating plan that you find intriguing?

___

5. Does your company currently measure its involvement in DEI?

___

JOURNAL SECTION

PART II

SUPPLIER DIVERSITY

"Economic inclusion may be the key to
lasting growth and prosperity."
— *Brookings*

CHANGE
DIVERSITY
INCLUSION
EQUITY
TEAM
people
racism
years
look
may
society
inequality
States
work
one
American
moment
white
time
power
supply
since
men
race
take
even
need
equal
Powell
last
fact
get
like
part
deep
help
Till
classism
areas
views

CHAPTER 4

KEY COMPONENTS OF YOUR SUPPLIER DIVERSITY STRATEGY

Despite the recent interest in workforce diversity initiatives, supplier diversity remains an area of focus for many corporations, nonprofits, and government entities. Corporations are setting ambitious goals to reach out to businesses not traditionally included in the supply chain. As it relates to supplier diversity, most business leaders invest in people they know. Procurement professionals have the daunting tasks of balancing pricing, quality products or services, and high service expectations. We need relationships to build allies for our business or career.

With any DEI strategic business strategy, having support for the senior executives, including the board of directors, is paramount. However, beyond the executive leaders of the organization, middle managers are required to buy in as well.

We need relationships to build allies for our business or career.

The reality is many, if not all of them, are making the final decisions anyway. Many corporations spend millions, even billions, of dollars a year on goods and services, yet historically, minority and women-owned businesses have been left behind in terms of securing supplier contracts with large corporations.

In response, supplier diversity programs have sprung up in companies of all industries and areas, and today, many companies are going beyond just utilizing minority and women-owned businesses. Companies are also considering the utilization of companies that are 51% owned, operating, and controlled by someone who is from the LGBTQ community or Veteran community. To ensure the successful execution of our supplier diversity strategy, it is necessary to consider muiltiple concepts.

Pre-sourcing

Relationships with sourcing professionals matter. They are looking to find the best suppliers at the best price, and that usually (not always) leads to them using suppliers they already know or are familiar with.

If you are a supplier diversity leader or just seeking to move the needle internally, you must understand the needs of the sourcing manager. Correctly matching diverse suppliers with procurement opportunities needs to be an ongoing and proactive process.

Forecasting purchasing requirements helps save time, reduce risks, and ensure diversity. Pre-sourcing is part of effective supply chain management and helps guarantee diverse suppliers get a fair opportunity to compete. When offered the chance to submit businesses for supplier consideration, make sure you have done the proper due diligence and put forth names that won't diminish your credibility.

Outreach

I understand that often it is convenient to use suppliers that you already know, but often those suppliers are not diverse and limit the opportunity to drive economic inclusion. Outreach is being very intentional about meeting a diverse range of suppliers that can give you competitive pricing, quality service, and reflect the communities your serve. An active approach to meeting diverse businesses is crucial to an effective supplier diversity strategy.

> *The great thing is you don't have to go at it alone.*

Whether virtual or in-person, effective ways to meet diverse companies include attending trade fairs, participating in local certification councils, attending chamber of commerce events, having a website, and advertising.

The great thing is you don't have to go at it alone. Partner with your supplier diversity director to make the proper introductions. Many times, they already know who and where the businesses are.

Before you get out there, make sure your internal affairs are in order. For example, do you have a page on your external site that allows businesses to register as suppliers? Do you have an updated supplier form that enables you to request the appropriate diversity certifications? Lastly, be sure your systems are set up to track spending with diverse companies. It does you little good to conduct outreach if your infrastructure isn't in place.

Goals

Setting quantifiable goals for making purchases from diverse businesses is critical to the success of any supplier diversity program. Goals set the necessary performance standards. Goals are established by benchmarking, spend opportunities, historical performance, and other demographic factors.

Be sure to set goals or "accountability metrics" at both the organizational and team level. This ensures shared ownership to reach your desired outcomes. Remember, this isn't about checking the box but driving economic inclusion that can give your company a competitive advantage in the market.

Goals set the necessary performance standards.

Tier 2

But what if you can't find diverse suppliers? Keep looking. That may mean you need to bolster your outreach efforts.

In all seriousness, you have several options to increase your spend:

1. Develop the suppliers you need (see chapter 6).
2. Establish a Tier 2 strategy. This strategy allows you to "encourage" (some would use the term "mandate") your non-minority suppliers to subcontract to diverse vendors. This can happen either directly or indirectly, in support of their contract with your organization.

Accountability

Managers and individual buyers across the organization must be held accountable for reaching supplier diversity goals. Again, what gets measured gets done. Sourcing or procurement professionals and end-users are measured in their performance review on cost savings and product/service quality. Supplier diversity should be included as a significant performance indicator as well.

Beneficial supplier diversity strategies include most, if not all, the program components listed above. However, best in class DEI strategies have an element of supplier diversity that focuses on the development of suppliers.

Earlier, I jokingly mentioned "that if you can't find a supplier, keep looking," but organizations that really focus on equity and inclusion build or develop what they can't find.

Sometimes it's not what you know or who you know; it is also who knows you. Whether you seek to advance your career or build a thriving enterprise as an entrepreneur, having mutually beneficial relationships matters! Building relationships takes time and should be grounded in trust.

Building relationships takes time and should be grounded in trust.

Our education or professional expertise is the foundation for the opportunities we are provided, but my experience as a corporate professional and business owner has taught me that the relationships we build can produce so many more opportunities to grow. Personal connections with managers, leaders, coworkers and customers can lead to increased employee engagement and performance.

Interestingly, people tend to build relationships with people in their proximity or those they have something in common with. So, if we are not in each other's "circle" or realize our commonalities, how do we go about building relationships?

Steps to Build Successful Relationships

Building relationships is the cornerstone for growth and success. If leveraged appropriately, relationships provide us the necessary structure to grow personally and professionally. These interactions should also be grounded in mutual trust and respect. To begin building or even nurturing relationships in your life or career, please consider the following:

- **Ask questions.** Over time, most people will share if you allow them space to do so. I have learned so much from business owners to CEOs just by asking questions. If you ask people about themselves, what they are working on, how you can help solve a problem and then take the time to listen attentively, you can build a genuine rapport over time.
- **Tell people about yourself.** People won't trust you unless you are willing to trust them. Tell them what you genuinely care about and what you think.

One of my favorite stories to share is why I am so passionate about my work. It's a story that dates back to high school and playing varsity football. I didn't take a chance on myself and said I would never let that happen again. While I played varsity football, I worked several jobs, so I didn't take my playing career very seriously. I was 5'8, less than 150 pounds. I was pretty small, but I was a student of the game.

Nonetheless, one day the coach called me into his office and told me that he was considering starting me at quarterback. I immediately said thanks, but no thanks. I assumed me being the starting quarterback might lead to someone else potentially losing a scholarship opportunity, so I declined.

I have been committed to maximizing my full potential no matter what it is I am doing.

The moral of the story is I have always wondered how successful we could have been as a team had I decided to lead as the quarterback. Not knowing has always haunted me, and from that day on, I have been committed to maximizing my full potential no matter what it is I am doing.

- **Go places and do things.** To maximize my full potential, I put myself in places that I wouldn't traditionally. This has allowed me to meet people I wouldn't typically meet.

  For example, I am a diversity professional, but I agree to serve on a public board that supports mobility and public transportation. I knew very little about public transit, but I have built long-standing, mutually beneficial relationships from this experience.

  It's not always at a supplier conference or the golf course. If you want to make friends and build relationships, you must go where the people are.

- **Learn about different cultures.** Even a tiny amount of effort will go a long way in showing that you care enough to find out about the reality of another person's life. If you are willing to take risks and put yourself in a situation where you might feel uncomfortable, people will be more inclined to want to get to know you.

- **Take a stand against oppression.** Actions speak louder than words. People who experience oppression need allies to help them push back against injustice. Strong relationships are forged when people act courageously on behalf of each other. If you hear or see something that is wrong…say something. Don't leave it up to someone else to address comments or behaviors that promote injustice or inequities.

- **Overcome fear of rejection.** Most of us suffer from a fear of rejection, and there's only one thing to do about it: get over it. If you want to form relationships, plan on being rejected. You will be richly rewarded the rest of the time with the new connections you have made.

Equally crucial to establishing relationships is maintaining them. Successful relationships involve active listening, being a resource to one another, and doing what you say you're going to do.

In order to get support from people outside our organizations, we need to build relationships in which people know and trust us. The more relationships you have, the better. Some relationships require more time than others. Take the time to get to know the organization, the person, or the people who you genuinely admire. You don't always need to want something in return.

Building relationships is the groundwork that must be laid before anything else gets done. When you plan to go after a business or build your career, you need to include the time it takes to build relationships in your plan. People need time to build trust.

> Some relationships require more time than others.

Whenever people work together, they need to have trusted relationships. When trust is missing, people usually have a difficult time functioning cooperatively. They worry about risking too much (this isn't you, is it?). Disagreements seem to erupt over no reason.

Investing time, resources, and one's organizational reputation can be risky. At the least, people want some return for their investment. They have to feel like you know them as a person, understand their interests, and will not let them down.

Building and sustaining relationships are at the heart of business and getting things done. The strength of community lies in the power of the connections that we have with each other.

With strong connections, people have the power to make real change. Building these connections takes time, but it is so worth it. As you invest in your career or business, remember to take time to nurture relationships because they matter. People support people they know and trust.

DEI GUIDED QUESTIONS

These questions are designed for you to reflect on what you read in this chapter and answer as appropriate.

1. Do you believe supplier diversity drives economic inclusion and strengthens our community?

2. Does your company track its spend with diverse businesses?

3. Have you been afforded an opportunity because of who you know?

4. Have you or someone you know been afforded an opportunity because of the network you or them previously built?

5. What percentage of career growth would you attribute to having successful relationships ____%?

JOURNAL SECTION

CHANGE
DIVERSITY
INCLUSION
EQUITY
TEAM
racism
people
years
look
may
society
workplace
america
inequality
States
moment
white
time
work
past
help
one
men
race
since
power
supply
take
even
equal
need
get
last
fact
Powell
areas
part
like
deep
big
views
now
racist
Till
classism
dates
life
names
American
act

CHAPTER 5

SUPPLIER DEVELOPMENT

How do you take your supplier diversity strategy to another level? Develop your diverse suppliers! This type of initiative can take time but can also pay big dividends in strengthening your supply chain. Procurement and sourcing teams are heavily reliant upon the effectiveness of the suppliers they choose to collaborate with.

Relationship management between buyer and supplier is crucial to a partnership's success rate, and both parties must learn to give and take to create a fair and shared value.

Supplier development is a business strategy that involves working with your diverse suppliers to boost their performance and drive continued business growth. Through education, mentoring, and access to resources, you'll help drive more sustainable and robust economic opportunities for your own business.

Whether you educate diverse suppliers on how you procure and your organizational needs, you'll help them access more vendors and foster competition between their suppliers. In addition to driving their growth, this optimization empowers suppliers to offer more competitive pricing, service levels, and options to your company. Some of the largest, most diverse businesses today grew through long-term sustainable relationships with majority-owned companies.

A supplier development program can provide much-needed additional support. Whether it's through education, mentoring, access to networks, access to capital, or all of the above, it allows a supplier the freedom to pursue new products and solutions and meet the needs of your organization.

By investing in your diverse suppliers' success and giving them opportunities to collaborate, you'll help grow your channels and sources. More supplier channels ultimately mean more companies competing for your business — and more options to choose from. With more options available, you can be more selective in your procurement decisions, receiving the best possible product and value.

Small, diverse suppliers often lack the resources or expertise to compete for large contracts on their own. A forward-thinking development program teaches suppliers with complementary solutions to form successful partnerships to win larger bids.

By investing in your diverse suppliers' development, you will also drive job creation and economic growth opportunities for local businesses and families. Along with boosting brand perception, creating more jobs strengthens the economy, which leads to more sourcing options for your organization down the line. Even more than supplier diversity programs, supplier development requires the support and involvement of your entire organization (beyond your procurement department).

Creating more jobs strengthens the economy.

Working one-on-one with suppliers—through mentor programs, for example—encourages C-suite and mid-level executives to become more intimately involved with these programs and aware of their benefits. This direct engagement will help improve buy-in for both supplier diversity and supplier development initiatives. Other initiatives that support supplier development include joint ventures and strategic partnerships.

Joint Venture

A joint venture is a child company of two parent companies. It is maintained by sharing resources and equity with a binding agreement. Whether it's formed for a specific purpose or an ongoing strategy, a joint venture has a clear objective, and profits are split between the two companies.

Strategic Partnerships

A venture that bolsters a core business strategy creates a competitive advantage and slows competitors from moving in on a marketplace. Both of the aforementioned partnerships can be formed with two minority companies or majority and minority companies. Each strategy creates scale and the ability to perform at a very high level.

The work of executing a best in class diversity and inclusion strategy is not an easy one! The main ingredient to ensuring sustainable success is accountability. Whether you are working with sourcing teams, hiring managers, or CEOs, there has to be accountability for what gets done and how change is made.

There is so much to gain from this approach to doing business.

I spent several years as a supplier diversity manager with two different companies. One of the strategic and impactful ways I saw diverse businesses grow and enter supply chains was through strategic partnerships and joint ventures.

There is so much to gain from this approach to doing business (i.e., economic inclusion, risky mitigation, scalability, etc.). It just takes motivation and a commitment to seeing diverse businesses succeed by having an opportunity to compete. LVMH, which owns Dom Pérignon and Moët & Chandon, now has a 50% stake in Jay-Z's champagne brand Armand de Brignac, also known as Ace of Spades. Sounds like an excellent joint venture to me.

DEI GUIDED QUESTIONS

1. In your current role, do you procure goods and services?

2. If so, do you attempt to identify diverse businesses?

3. What do you believe is the most significant barrier for diverse businesses?

4. Does your organization have diverse strategic partnerships or joint ventures?

5. If you started a company today (or have a company), who could/should you partner with?

JOURNAL SECTION

DIVERSITY
INCLUSION
CHANGE
TEAM
EQUITY
racism
years
look
may
people
American
equal
need
fact
last
get
Powell
even
moment
white
time
work
one
States
inequality
help
supply
power
society
workplace
America
since
race
men
take
views
like
deep
part
areas
classism
Till
dates
1866
67
20105
2009
1950
1979
1920
150
10450
20106

PART III

ACCOUNTABILITY

"Personal accountability requires mindfulness, acceptance, honesty, and courage."
— *Shelby Martin*

CHANGE
DIVERSITY
INCLUSION
EQUITY
TEAM
people
years
racism
look
may
American
moment
equal
need
Powell
even
take
big
society
States
inequality
workplace
america
since
power
supply
race
men
one
work
time
past
white
part
like
deep
help
Till
last
fact
fami
areas
views
classism
dates
act
2009
1950
1979
1920
1866
67
150
20105
20106
10450
400
20219
20158

CHAPTER 6

ESTABLISHING ACCOUNTABILITY METRICS

Have you heard the phrase, "What gets measured gets done"? Sure, you have! Creating specific goals for diversity and inclusion can mean various things. They can be a particular demographic that you are looking to increase or a change in a process.

DEI goals can also mean a complete overhaul of your values or changes in hiring strategies. An annual goal-setting process takes a data analytical approach to establish appropriate workforce and supplier goals/accountability metrics at the organization and department levels. Below is a mock schedule to consider and the stakeholders that should be included in the process.

Step 1: Schedule meetings with business unit/department leaders in August. Usually, you're trying to coordinate a ton of calendars for a one-hour session. Do not underestimate this process. Not getting the meetings scheduled promptly can set the entire schedule back by weeks, maybe even months. Proper planning promotes good performance!

Step 2: Review and analyze a full year of supplier spend and workforce data in August as well. While meetings are being scheduled, begin working with your analytics team to look at your supplier and workforce data. Yes, you will be having two conversations at once. You want to establish the appropriate accountability metrics for each strategic objective (e.g., workforce, supplier diversity). Typical datasets might include new hires, overall workforce demographics, overall spend, and diversity spend. Always use your data to tell the story.

Step 3: Meet with internal stakeholders to plan (i.e., finance, sourcing, HR business partner) in September. I've never really been a big fan of scheduling a meet-

> *Proper planning promotes good performance!*

ing to prepare for the meeting, but this calls for it. When you meet with the head of your CEO's business lines, you need to be in lockstep with all of your partners. You need to know the data inside and out, so meeting to ensure proper alignment is essential.

Step 4: Meet with business leaders to review progress and set goals/metrics in November. Be patient! You may not lock in your goals during this meeting, but the more prepared you are, the better. Negotiating isn't bad here either, but don't be afraid to stretch the organization. You can never advance the way you want to if you aren't bold and aggressive. Make the goals attainable but not easy.

> *You can never advance the way you want to if you aren't bold and aggressive.*

Step 5: Finalize business unit goals and metrics in late November and December. Remember you are setting goals by each business line/department, ultimately leading to the organization's goals. Once you have all goals locked in, be sure to add them to your DEI scorecard and socialize with your internal stakeholders.

Step 6: Finalize organizational goals and metrics and communicate to your board of directors in December. Organizationally, this is the highest level of accountability you can promote.

Be sure the board has full transparency of your workforce and supplier diversity goals and make a point to share successes with them quarterly.

As we discussed earlier, any dependable business plan has quantifiable measures to ensure growth. DEI is no different. Organizational leaders should consider establishing accountability metrics (goals) to provide a diverse and inclusive workforce and supplier base. The process outlined above should be supported by data analytics but is designed to revisit the gaps that may exist within your organization and promote having a comprehensive discussion on how you can close those gaps.

Setting accountability metrics can be very arduous, time-consuming, and take a bit of negotiating. However, now that you have a public statement on DEI and an operating plan, you have to ensure that what you seek to improve (workforce diversity or community engagement) is actually advancing. The targets you set should not be designed to force undesired behavior but promote shared accountability in addressing a company's business strategy. A very effective way to promote shared accountability is to create an internal DEI Advisory Council.

DEI GUIDED QUESTIONS

These questions are designed for you to reflect on what you read in this chapter and answer as appropriate.

1. Do you have any performance goals? Are DEI metrics a part of your goals?

___

2. Are DEI goals tied to incentive compensation?

___

3. Does your organization have a DEI scorecard/dashboard to measure success?

___

4. Is DEI an agenda item for your board of directors?

___

5. Does your executive team have monthly discussions regarding your organizational progress?

___

JOURNAL SECTION

CHANGE
DIVERSITY
INCLUSION
TEAM
EQUITY
racism
years
look
may
people
American
equal
moment
inequality
States
workplace
society
power
supply
since
America
race
one
work
time
past
help
need
fact
last
get
even
Powell
white
areas
take
views
like
deep
part
men
go
act
big
racist
now
Till
classism
dates
life
1950
2009
20158
1920
1979
150
10450
1866
67
20105
20106
400

CHAPTER 7

ESTABLISH AN INTERNAL DIVERSITY ADVISORY COUNCIL

Most organizations only have one to two full-time staff dedicated to DEI. Therefore, it is essential to build allies and partners throughout the organization who can help promote shared accountability.

There are usually only one or two people assigned to focus on DEI as part of their full-time job. This is a very daunting task because DEI touches every single aspect of your organization. I found it very beneficial to extend the work of the DEI team by establishing a group of leaders who can champion the work within the respective business unit.

During each goal-setting meeting with executive leaders, I would ask them to appoint someone from their team to serve on the council to help with our collective enhancement. Below are critical components of establishing an internal DEI Advisory Council.

Mission

Your mission should remind your council why DEI is important and align with the organization's overall mission. This helps keep your work connected to the hearts and minds of all your internal stakeholders.

Create an environment where everyone has equal opportunities, stimulates innovation, presents new approaches, and brings fresh perspectives that allow us to expand our work into more diverse communities and make a meaningful impact in others' lives.

Objectives

Your objectives give the group focus and direction. This group's objectives should align with your DEI operating plan and provide the team members a platform for discussion and progress measurement.

This is a very daunting task because DEI touches every single aspect of your organization.

- Ensure alignment and adherence to the advisory council guidelines.

- Be a resource to help advance the mission and goals of the diversity, equity, and inclusion strategy.

The advisory council plays a critical role in supporting the achievement of the diversity, equity, and inclusion strategy. Additionally, the council can:

- Provide an opportunity for all colleagues to be a part of creating an inclusive culture.
- Organize and promote activities to increase awareness of DEI.
- Act as a sounding board for strategic diversity and inclusion objectives that affect colleagues in the office/region to advance the diversity and inclusion strategy.
- Support volunteer efforts that align with the DEI strategy.

Operating Principles

These principles should guide how the group operates.

- All members should have equal access to data and the ability to provide input into the strategic direction of the DEI strategy.
- The advisory council should have a very strategic focus on forward-thinking objectives and expansion.
- Advisory council members and participants should reflect on each department or business unit.

Roles and Responsibilities

The advisory council format should execute the business case for DEI and extend the organizational reach by increasing shared responsibility. The council meetings should provide an ongoing platform to discuss strategic objectives, development, challenges, and goal attainment. Additionally, the council should meet at least four times a year.

DEI Advisory Council Membership

Council leader:

- This role is usually held by a direct report of your CEO.
- Communicate the council's mission and objectives both internally and externally.
- Provide input for measuring the council's effectiveness and identifying improvement opportunities.

Advisory council members:

- Members should reflect on each department of the organization.
- Be able to communicate your DEI strategic direction, progress, and challenges.
- Provide oversight, guidance, and support for sustainability efforts, performance, and risks.
- Provide input for measuring the council's effectiveness and identifying improvement opportunities.

Councils must clearly link the organization's diversity strategy with the overall business strategy to emphasize the importance of diversity in and to the organization. It is not enough for an organization to say, "We should look more diverse because customers like that." Rather, it's important to ask, "How can we better reflect our diverse customer base, thus providing them with better service, care, and products?"

Many diversity councils are designed to address gaps in representation or inclusion for specific demographic groups, including women, racially/ethnically diverse individuals, and people with disabilities. Other councils address diversity and inclusion more broadly and consider every member to represent some aspect of diversity: dimensions may include organizational role or level, educational background, communication or management style, geographic location, and demographic group.

A diversity council's members should mirror the diversity within the organization. Councils should be composed of individuals of different genders, generations, departments, and other dimensions of diversity. Leaders of employee resource groups may also be part of the council. Councils may include individuals with diversity expertise who do not work for the organization; these outsiders can provide expertise or offer a customer's perspective in council discussions.

It is vital to have the right people involved on the DEI Advisory Council. The typical council member is a well-connected, very well-respected, highly influential leader. He or she has a great deal of knowledge regarding the organization itself, the challenges and issues associated with specific business units, and has intimate knowledge of the concerns associated with how work gets done.

A diversity council's members should mirror the diversity within the organization.

As a group, the DEI Advisory Council reflects a balanced representation of the business. The organization's leaders work side-by-side with council members to ensure that the overall business plan is fully aligned with the diversity and inclusion strategy.

Through the work of the councils, leaders co-create diversity and inclusion

Establish an Internal Diversity Advisory Council

goals, monitor outcomes and strategy execution, and report progress to company leaders and the organization overall.

DEI GUIDED QUESTIONS

These questions are designed for you to reflect on what you read in this chapter and answer as appropriate.

1. Does your organization have full-time DEI staff or an internal advisory council?

_____

_____

_____

2. Is your council comprised of a cross section of organizational leaders?

_____

_____

_____

3. In what ways can organizations promote shared accountability for DEI?

_____

_____

_____

4. If your organization had an advisory council, would you volunteer to serve on it?

_____

_____

_____

5. Does your advisory council leverage subcommittees to support the execution of your DEI strategy?

_____

_____

_____

JOURNAL SECTION

CHANGE DIVERSITY TEAM INCLUSION

racism, equity, inequality, states, society, American, workplace, power, people, work, time, moment, years, look, change, team, diversity, inclusion, equality, race, white, men, life, help, supply, family, need, equal, Powell, Till, America, since, classism, past, areas, views, take, may, one, get, deep, like, act, United, part, big, racist, fact, moment

CHAPTER 8
CELEBRATE PROGRESS

Hey! Make no mistake about it. The work of DEI is hard work! Therefore, when you have success and wins (no matter how big or small), it is vital to take time to celebrate them. Celebration breeds more success and adds to the satisfaction you experience when you note your accomplishments in the workplace.

When you onboard a new diverse supplier, hire an executive African American woman, or are recognized by Forbes for being one of America's top companies for diversity — celebrate.

There will be pitfalls in the process, but that shouldn't stop you from celebrating every success along the way. We all set goals for ourselves and work hard to achieve those goals. Recognizing and celebrating success is a potent motivator for individuals and teams because it reinforces the meaning behind all that hard work, and it shows appreciation for the achievements.

This, in turn, boosts confidence and motivates us to take the next step toward achieving the next goal. While you know you need to praise successes, sometimes the how is elusive.

There will be pitfalls in the process, but that shouldn't stop you from celebrating every success along the way.

While celebrations need to reflect your company culture and the degree and contribution of the success, these ideas will help you start celebrating success at work.

Some examples of celebration are verbal praise, writing recognition, or a recognition event.

Verbal Praise

Sometimes just saying, "Thank you. You did a terrific job," can validate your workers. Providing this feedback in public or private settings can provide positive reinforcement while enhancing the celebration and an employee's feeling of recognition.

Although it may seem a little impersonal, even voicemail messages can go a long way. There's nothing like picking up the phone to let someone know they've done a job well done, and you're taking time to acknowledge it.

Written Recognition

A kind email to the individual can go a long way. An email to the whole group praising an employee's success can go even further. An email to an entire team that celebrates their success is amazingly effective in influencing future employee behavior and contributions.

When you think about the work it takes to make progress with DEI, you will realize it takes a myriad of people and teams to move in the right direction. Most goals are set at the department or business line level.

As you see growth, be sure to let the department head and team know their efforts are recognized. I also recommend including written recognition in an internal newsletter or monthly report.

Hold a Recognition Event/Awards Ceremony

A good practice is to establish specific awards for workforce and supplier diversity. You can present awards for individuals or teams, even both. Suppose you decided to establish an internal Advisory Council. In that case, you may want to use the first meeting of the year to recognize those who helped you accelerate your DEI initiative the previous year.

Be sure to invite your CEO, executives, and leadership members from your business resource groups. And because this is a big deal, invest a few dollars in a plaque or trophy (wink).

After you recognize your colleagues at your formal event, be sure to share the winners on your intranet site. Make it a big deal! And when you receive external awards, be sure to post those on your external website as well. These are significant recruiting and branding tools for your organization. Celebrating the small wins is actually a very powerful motivating factor. Sharing our stories of overcoming and achievement inspires those around us to "find their why."

> *Celebrating the small wins is actually a very powerful motivating factor.*

As we continue to go through tough economic times and racial disparities in our communities, workplace, and health systems, take some time out to appreciate your efforts and of those around you.

DEI GUIDED QUESTIONS

These questions are designed for you to reflect on what you read in this chapter and answer as appropriate.

1. Do you recognize progress at work? If so, how?

   _____

   _____

   _____

2. Does your organization have internal DEI awards?

   _____

   _____

   _____

3. Do your employees understand the criteria associated with being recognized for DEI?

   _____

   _____

   _____

4. Does your organization recognize your suppliers for their commitment to DEI?

   _____

   _____

   _____

5. Has a third party recognized your organization for your progress with DEI?

   _____

   _____

   _____

JOURNAL SECTION

CHANGE
DIVERSITY
INCLUSION
EQUITY
TEAM
racism
years
look
may
people
American
moment
equal
need
Powell
fact
last
get
even
take
big
racist
now
views
society
power
supply
America
since
workplace
Till
classism
dates
States
inequality
help
work
time
past
one
men
go
race
part
act
like
deep
white
areas
life
1950
2009
20158
1920
1979
10450
150
1866
67
20105
20106
400

CHAPTER 9

BENCHMARK BEST IN CLASS STRATEGIES AND INITIATIVES

Mature DEI strategies can take anywhere from three to five years to evolve. Celebrate your victories along the way, but always have an eye on the future.

If you have a colleague engagement survey, create a DEI Index to measure your accomplishments and learn what opportunities still exist within your organization. Your company should always seek to get better.

Continuous Improvement

Initiatives throughout your plan should address gaps between your current state on DEI and desired state. The process to ensure that you maintain the right DEI strategy to support your business is a continuous cycle that must be performed frequently.

In support of our continuous improvement process, consider performing all or a combination of the following on an annual basis:

- Meet and obtain feedback from colleagues and internal stakeholders.
- Benchmark against companies that are best in class in DEI.
- Solicit feedback from our suppliers and community stakeholders.

Obtain Feedback

Feedback from internal stakeholders is an excellent way to assess your progression along the DEI journey. Your colleagues will definitely let you know how they feel about your workforce demographics, especially in senior management roles and your culture. Focus groups or regular team meetings can provide you an opportunity to hear how they feel. If you are requesting feedback, be sure to create a safe space for your colleagues to be open and honest.

Focus groups or regular team meetings can provide you an opportunity to hear how they feel.

Benchmarking
It is a decent idea to benchmark your development, policies, and procedures with third-party organizations. Benchmarking outside your industry is a fantastic way to get breakthrough results.

Below are a few organizations with very mature assessment processes and are well recognized in the DEI industry:

DiversityInc Top 50 Companies for Diversity
The DiversityInc Top 50 Companies for Diversity is globally the leading assessment of diversity management. The survey assesses companies in six key areas of diversity and inclusion: human capital diversity metrics, leadership accountability, talent programs, workplace practices, supplier diversity, and philanthropy.

Human Rights Campaign Corporate Equality Index
Human Rights Campaign Foundation's Corporate Equality Index is the national benchmarking tool on corporate policies and practices pertinent to lesbian, gay, bisexual, and transgender employees.

Military Friendly Employers
The list of Military Friendly® Employers distinguishes elite companies who boast the most substantial job opportunities, hiring practices, and retention programs for transitioning service members and spouses seeking civilian employment.

After you complete the surveys you deem appropriate for your organization, go back and revisit your responses. For questions you had to answer "no" or "not applicable," those may be areas of opportunity for continuous improvement.

Remember, building a world-class DEI strategy takes time, but with each year, you should move closer and closer to having a work environment that is diverse, equitable, and inclusive. Remember, if leveraged effectively, this strategic business imperative (DEI) can give you a competitive advantage over your competitors.

Feedback from External Stakeholders

Another great way to learn what others think about your organization's DEI efforts is to ask your suppliers or community stakeholders. Trust me. They will tell you what they think and what the market is saying. Most external stakeholders want to see companies improve their DEI strategies, and sometimes will be very critical. Try not to take unfavorable feedback personally. Instead, use it to get better.

Try not to take unfavorable feedback personally.

Whether you seek input from internal/external stakeholders or benchmark against industry leaders, be sure to communicate areas where you have improved. Remember, executing a DEI strategy is a journey. It takes time.

There will be highs and lows throughout the process, but if your organization and you as an individual understand and embrace the importance of this work, you will be proud of the progress you make. And you should be proud!

DEI GUIDED QUESTIONS

These questions are designed for you to reflect on what you read in this chapter and answer as appropriate.

1. Does your organization complete DEI benchmarking surveys?

_____
_____
_____

2. Does your organization use the results from benchmarking surveys to improve your strategy?

_____
_____
_____

3. How can benchmarking help your organization improve DEI outcomes?

_____
_____
_____

4. Has your organization identified surveys that will help you improve your DEI strategy?

_____
_____
_____

5. Do you have dedicated internal resources to complete external benchmarking surveys?

_____
_____

JOURNAL SECTION

DIVERSITY
INCLUSION
CHANGE
TEAM
EQUALITY
people
years
racism
look
may
take
equal
need
last
fact
get
even
American
Powell
moment
white
time
work
one
men
race
States
inequality
society
since
workplace
America
power
supply
help
like
deep
act
part
views
big
racist
now
areas
Till
classism
dates
2009
1950
1920
1979
150
1866
67
20105

CONCLUSION

This book introduced you to noteworthy concepts that can help you and your organization succeed in DEI. Through it, I hope I've helped you understand how to create a workforce or supplier base that reflects the changing demographics, is inclusive, drives economic inclusion, and closes the income and health inequality gaps.

To achieve equity, we are required to take awareness to action and work diligently to mitigate bias and root out the racism that lives within our systems, workforce, housing, and criminal justice, to education, the economy, and health care. You'll notice in this chapter I say 'we,' and by 'we,' I mean all of us.

The disparities and inequality that we see today are linked to our country's early beginning. Let's face it; our country was founded on principles designed to leave out underrepresented groups. This systematic modeling creates a roadblock for ethnic minorities, women, immigrants, LGBT+ people, poor people, and those with disabilities that the majority will never face, such as the reality that blacks weren't even considered humans by some people.

Acknowledging this sobering reality requires an understanding that inequality results from unequal structures and systems, not cultural deficits or a lack of personal responsibility. We all need intrinsic motivation or self-awareness to see a more inclusive and equitable society. One that allows all of us the opportunity to create generational advancement, opportunity, and wealth.

> As business leaders, we need to use our privilege and power to implement transformative change.

As business leaders, we need to use our privilege and power to implement transformative change. This means holding bad actors and institutions accountable, redistributing resources to communities that have historically been left behind, and fighting for more equitable systems that authentically include, center, and elevate marginalized voices. Words of support mean little without real accountability and action.

Diversity, equity, and inclusion are not just buzz words. They are the guiding ideas that will lead to a more equal society. Creating a diverse and inclusive workplace requires us to take ownership of creating a competitive, innovative, and empowering approach environment for all to succeed. So, as you set on your DEI journey, or continue your DEI journey, remember to establish a DEI operating plan that serves as your playbook for success.

This plan should include meaningful components that address representation and inclusion. Remember, early on in your plan, you should have your DEI statement. This stated commitment is what you want your employees, customers, and the community to know about your commitment to DEI. After your stated commitment, clearly lay out your strategic objectives for DEI. These are the areas where you'll want to focus your attention daily. Remember, what gets measured should get done, so be bold and aggressive. Establish metrics that will hold internal stakeholders accountable for attainment.

While DEI training is crucial, it is not the panacea for this work. Training should be a supplement to key objectives and initiatives. Don't be shy about relying on your affinity groups to keep a pulse on how you're moving the needle within the company.

Remember, what gets measured should get done, so be bold and aggressive.

They will let you know everything you need to know about how you're doing. Your affinity groups are a wonderful resource for impacting policy change and a great way to ensure equity as you are working on your diverse pipeline, leverage colleagues' referrals. They can sometimes be the best recruiter. Hold your search firms accountable for bringing your diverse candidates to consider. And partner with various organizations committed to DEI. Historically Black Colleges and Universities (HBCUs) are a superb pipeline and resource for a diverse talent pool.

Communication is key. If your advocates or champions don't know what you're doing, they can't support you. Communicate often. Also, take moments to celebrate different cultures and traditions within your organization. I would recommend setting a monthly calendar that allows you to highlight diversity. This could include celebrating Juneteenth or National Women's History Month.

Supplier Diversity is a fundamental strategic objective of any world-class DEI strategy. Be sure to make this a priority by engaging your sourcing team early and often.

Lastly, celebrate the big and small. If you bring on a new diverse supplier or rank #1 as the best place in American for diversity, celebrate. This is challenging and oftentimes thankless work, so celebrating wins is a formidable motivating factor.

As we continue to go through tough economic times and racial disparities in our communities and workplace, take time out to appreciate your efforts and those around you. Remember, diversity starts with you!

CHANGE DIVERSITY EQUITY INCLUSION TEAM

IDEAS TO CREATE AN INCLUSIVE AND EQUITABLE WORKPLACE

Starting and sustaining a DEI strategy takes a lot of work and requires engagement at all levels of the organization. Remember, attracting diverse talent is requisite, but keeping them at your organization and creating an environment where they feel welcomed is even better.

There are several ways that you can build an inclusive culture. As stated throughout this guide, it begins with having a plan. Impactful DEI strategies will always require a balance of bold initiatives, but the subtle considerations and activities can have an equally important impact within your organization. Consider these 20 initiatives that you could execute immediately to begin building an inclusive culture.

1. **Put your organizational culture on display.** Make an effort to put up signage or artifacts that promote the values you want your colleagues to feel or think. Identifying cultural artifacts can be a quick way to understanding how a team works and what they believe.

2. **What does your company look like to others?** When people are considering new opportunities, one of the first places they go for information is your website. Take a fresh look at the visuals of your careers page. What demographics are represented in your photos? In your leadership bios? Candidates may interpret a non-diverse careers page as a sign of a non-inclusive workplace.

3. **Convert job descriptions to gender-neutral language.** Audit all of your job descriptions to check for any use of 'he/his/him' as a default and convert them to gender-neutral pronouns like 'he or she' or 'they.'

4. **Mitigate bias in the resume review process.** Conduct blind screenings to limit stereotyping potential talent based on 'ethnic' names. You may want to consider removing all names and focusing on the credentials of the candidate.

5. **Write results-based job descriptions.** Studies have found that men apply for a job when they meet only 60 percent of the qualifications, but women will only apply when they meet 100 percent. Instead of being based on a checklist of skills that may weed out notable female and minority candidates, job descriptions should ideally focus on what a candidate will be expected to achieve, in say, a month, six months, and a year into the job.

6. **Create a pipeline of diverse talent.** If you want to see better representation, you have to expand your reach/network. Challenge your employees to think beyond the obvious — past their three best friends that may or may not be all from the same demographic. Emphasize that diversity requires deliberate effort, and it's something all employees can help with — by making introductions to remarkable people they know. Make it a point to meet at least two or three talented individuals a month. You can also enhance this process by getting to know the diverse talent in your own organization.

7. **Invest in a structured interviewing process and training.** This isn't to say that you must stick to a strict script in your interviews — candidates often share important insights when conversations flow naturally — but structured interviews lead to higher-quality hires because they help reduce bias and "gut-feeling" hiring. By asking each candidate the same or a similar set of questions, you have a consistent "data set" to help boost objective decision-making. Structured interviews will allow your team to learn and improve your recruiting process faster, as well.

8. **Diversify your interview teams.** I can't stress this point enough; you have to be purposeful in ensuring that underrepresented employees are included in your interviews. Yes, diverse candidates want to see diverse faces, but you also want diversity on both sides of the table. Even if the candidate is not diverse, having a diverse colleague communicate the importance of this work could add significant value to the conversation.

9. **Make sure DEI is integrated into your onboarding process.** Include things like your DEI commitment statement and maybe a short video that clearly

Ideas to Create an Inclusive and Equitable Workplace

welcomes the new colleague and explains why DEI is indispensable to your organization. This is important to ensure shared accountability at all levels of the company.

10. **Consider flexible work hours.** Show your employees you trust them to get their work done with the freedom to create their own work hours. People have all sorts of personal situations that may affect their ability to work a strict 9 to 5 (like picking up or dropping off children at school). Lack of flexibility makes the lives of some employees unnecessarily difficult, and they may respond by leaving for a company that does. We all want to retain our best talent.

11. **Make your expectations clear.** Highlight your inclusive leadership behaviors and be sure to post them so they are visible and serve as a reminder of how every colleague can contribute to an inclusive workplace.

12. **Establish a mother's room if you don't currently have one.** Creating a private space where nursing mothers can pump breast milk is a valuable accommodation.

13. **Invite a guest speaker from the DEI community** to speak at your company. Especially if you already have regular talks on technical topics or leadership — just set aside a couple of slots for DEI. This is also an effective way to benchmark your internal progress.

14. **Establish a parental leave policy.** Policies to support parents and caregivers can play a massive part in making a workplace more inclusive, not to mention more attractive to candidates. This is becoming increasingly pertinent in the decision-making process for choosing a company to work for.

15. **Partner with nonprofits and community organizations.** Chose an organization that aligns with your commitment to DEI and build a partnership. For example, if you are a financial institution, you may want to consider providing a financial empowerment series for students at historically black colleges and universities. Reach out to organizations that support economic inclusion offer to support their mission.

16. **Include DEI in performance conversations.** If you're not tying DEI directly to individual goals, you can still touch upon hiring managers' efforts, reach, and the expectations you have for them in performance conversations.

17. **Provide learning and development workshops.** These are wonderful for developing skills like communication and empathy for employees. An inclusive workforce is an emotionally intelligent one that leverages self-awareness to improve relationships throughout the organization.

18. **Encourage your leaders to get involved in the dialogue.** If you are a leader in an organization, your colleagues want to hear from you. Don't shy away from joining in on the discussion. Sometimes the conversations will be challenging, but your colleagues will appreciate you more when it's over. Be willing to share articles, post on social media, or join crucial conversations on this topic. Silence can be deafening.

19. **Recognize your colleagues.** Contributing to your workplace isn't just hitting sales goals or creating new products — it's also doing your part to make your organization the best place that your colleagues have ever worked. I think that's worth recognizing. Think about creating a monthly newsletter that highlights the work by your colleagues to improve inclusion and build equity.

20. **Celebrate cultural holidays and heritage months for underrepresented groups** like Dewali, Juneteenth, or Asian Pacific American Heritage Month (May).

Don't try to change the company all at once. Start small. Build momentum and consistently check in with your colleagues to understand the impact of the things you are doing. Don't let the intensity of things that need to be done keep you from doing anything at all. You can talk about DEI forever, but taking action will create the change you want to see. Diversity starts with you!

KEY TERMS

Accountability Metrics: Agreed upon targets for ensuring growth in hiring and retention or contracting with diverse companies or other components are your DEI strategy that you want to measure to drive performance.

Affinity Groups: Sometimes referred to as business resource groups (BRGs) or employee resources groups (ERGs). These groups are formed by a shared interest, common goal, or dimension of diversity.

Causal Attributions: The process by which people begin to explain the causes of behavior and events.

Consciousness: Focused attention that aims outward toward the environment.

Continuous Improvement: An effort to improve processes, procedures, and strategy.

DEI: A commonly used acronym to describe diversity, equity, and inclusion.

Empowerment: Providing someone the opportunity to feel included or engaged in a process or system. This is instrumental behavior in a team setting.

Historically Black College or University (HBCU): Institutions of higher learning in education established to primarily serve the African American community.

Humility: An attitude of modesty that comes from understanding our place in the larger order of things. Consistently valuing the social good over the satisfaction of individual aspirations.

Insight: The capacity to understand the psychological functioning of self and others.

Intrinsic Motivation: Behavior that is driven by internal reward or gratification.

Job Flexibility: Describes the level of autonomy and control one has in the workplace regarding time or work location.

Pre-sourcing: Taking the time to identify a supplier to work with as a part of your supply chain. Serves as a triage process for understanding business needs and potential opportunities to meet new suppliers.

Self-awareness: The ability to make meaning of environmental stimuli and the impact on one's inner self.

Stability: A dimension of attribution described as the perceived variability or permanence of related incidents.

Supplier Diversity: A strategic business imperative that drives economic inclusion by spending dollars with minority-owned companies.

Supplier Development: Assisting a company with the tools and resources needed to grow in size or their ability to service new or existing business customers.

Tier 2: A key component of a supplier diversity strategy that brings two companies together in a business relationship to meet the customer's business needs.

Trait Desirability: Traits or characteristics that are directly associated with effective leadership.

Worldview: The personal values, ideals, or belief system that contribute to how someone sees things around them.

BIBLIOGRAPHY

Boyatzis, R. E., Stubbs, E. C., & Taylor, S. N. (2002). Learning cognitive and emotional intelligence competencies through graduate management education. *Academy of Management Learning and Education*, *1*, 150-162. DOI: 10.5465/AMLE.2002.8509345 10.1207/s15327752jpa4806_10

Bureau of Labor Statistics (2006). Charting the U.S. Labor Market in 2006; Retrieved from http://www.bls.gov/cps/labor2006/home.htm

Caruso, D. R., Mayer, J. D., & Salovey, P. (2002). Relation of an ability measure of emotional intelligence to personality. *Journal of Personality Assessment, 79, 306-320.*

Deloitte (2017). Unleashing human potential. Retrieved from https://www2.deloitte.com/us/en/pages/about-deloitte/solutions/diversity-inclusion-strategy-services.html.

Duval, T.S., & Lalwani, N. (1999). Objective self-awareness and causal attributions for self- standard discrepancies: Changing self or changing standards of correctness. *Personality and Social Psychology Bulletin*, *25*(10), 1220-1229. doi:10.1177/0146167299258004

Duvall, S., & Wicklund, R.A., (1972). *A theory of objective self-awareness.* New York, NY: Academic Press.

Economic Policy Institute (2011). Upper Tail inequality growing steadily: Men's wage inequality, 1973-2009. Retrieved from http://www.stateofworkingamerica.org/charts/view/192.

Economix (2010). The Value of College. Retrieved from https://economix.blogs.nytimes.com/2010/05/17/the-value-of-college-2/

Goleman, D. (1995). *Emotional intelligence.* New York, NY: Bantam.

Goleman, D. (1998). *Working with emotional intelligence.* New York, NY: Bantam.

Goleman, D. (2004). What makes a leader? *Harvard Business Review, 82*(1), 82-91.

John Powell (2021). Asians must be a part of our story, too. Retrieved from https://belonging.berkeley.edu/asians-must-be-part-our-story-too

Kondrat, M.E. (1999). Who is the self in self-aware: Professional self-awareness from a critical theory perspective. *Social Service Review, 73*(4), 451-477.

Lord, R.G., Foti, R.J. & De Vader, C.L. (1984). A test of leadership categorization theory:

Internal structure, information processing, and leadership perceptions. *Organizational Behavior & Human Performance,* 34(3), 343-378.

Lord, R.G. (1985). An information processing approach to social perceptions, leadership perceptions, and behavioral measurement in organizations. In B.M. Staw, & L.L. Cummings (Eds.). *Research in Organizational Behavior, 7,* 87-128.

Nichols, A.L., & Cottrell, C. A. (2014). What do people desire in their leaders? The role of leadership level on trait desirability. *The Leadership Quarterly, 25*(4), 711-729.

NPR (2021). Biden Takes Office. Retrieved from https://www.npr.org/sections/president-biden-takes-office/2021/02/05/963837953/biden-pledged-historic-cabinet-diversity-heres-how-his-nominees-stack-up.

Schermerhorn, C. (2015). The Business of Slavery and the Rise of American Capitalism, 1815–1860. New Haven, CT: Yale University Press

Showry, M., & Manasa, K. L. (2014). Self-Awareness — Key to Effective Leadership. *IUP Journal of Soft Skills*, *13*(1), 15-26.

Urdang, E. (2010). Awareness of Self — A Critical Tool. *Social Work Education*, *29*(5), 523-538.

Western, Bruce & Becky Pettit (2010). Incarceration and Social Inequality. Daedalus, 139(3), 8-19.

Made in the USA
Coppell, TX
20 February 2023